Windows

Also by Robert Creeley

POETRY

For Love
Words
The Charm
Pieces
A Day Book
Selected Poems
Hello: A Journal
Later
Collected Poems 1945–1975
Mirrors
Memory Gardens

FICTION

The Gold Diggers
The Island
Presences
Mabel: A Story
Collected Prose

DRAMA

Listen

ESSAYS

A Quick Graph: Collected Notes & Essays
Was That a Real Poem & Other Essays
Collected Essays

ANTHOLOGIES AND SELECTIONS

The Black Mountain Review 1954–1957
New American Story (with Donald M. Allen)
The New Writing in the U.S.A. (with Donald M. Allen)
Selected Writings of Charles Olson
Whitman: Selected Poems
The Essential Burns

Robert Creeley

Windows

A NEW DIRECTIONS BOOK

Acknowledgments: Grateful acknowledgment is made to the editors and publishers of magazines, newspapers, chapbooks, postcards, and anthologies in which many of the poems in this collection first appeared. Mazagines and newspapers: *A Dog's Nose, Arete, Black Mountain II Review, Blue Mesa Review, Bombay Gin, Boundary 2, Caliban, Conjunctions, Credences, Cutbank, Exquisite Corpse, Forbes, Giants Play Well in the Drizzle, Harvard Magazine, Human Means, Infolio, In Relation, Acts 10, Jerusalem Post, Literaturalmanach, manuskripte: Zeitschrift for Literatur, Napalm Health Spa, Notus, Nuori Voima, o•blēk, Organic Gardening, Painted Bride Quarterly, The Poetry Project, River Styx, Sagetrieb, Salt Lick Magazine, The Taos Review, Temblor, Western Humanities Review.* Chapbooks: *The Company* (Burning Deck Press, 1988); *Dreams* (Periphery & The Salient Seedling Press, 1989); *7 & 6* (Hoshour Gallery, Albuquerque, 1988); *Window: Paintings by Martha Visser't Hooft, Poems by Robert Creeley* (The Poetry/Rare Book Collection, State University of New York at Buffalo, 1988). Postcards: "Spring Light" (Limberlost Press, 1990). Anthologies: *Poets for Life: Seventy-six Poets Respond to AIDS,* ed. Michael Klein (Crown, 1989); *The Green American Tradition,* ed. H. Daniel Peck (Louisiana State University Press, 1989); *Louis Zukofsky, or Whoever Someone Else Thought He Was: A Collection of Responses to the Work of Louis Zukofsky,* ed. Harry Gilonis (North And South, 1988).

Eight poems from the sequence "Eight Plus" were engraved on the bollards at Seventh and Figueroa, Los Angeles, dated July 20, 1988, by the Seventh Street Plaza Associates in co-operation with The Prudential Realty Group.

The epigraph for the section "Helsinki Window," from Malcolm Lowry's *Dark As the Grave Wherein My Friend Is Laid* (NAL, 1968) is reprinted by permission of Sterling Lord Literistic, Inc., Copyright © 1968 by Margerie Bonner Lowry.

Manufactured in the United States of America
New Directions Books are printed on acid-free paper.
First published clothbound and as New Directions Paperbook 687 in 1990
Published simultaneously in Canada by Penguin Books Canada Limited

Library of Congress Cataloging in Publication Data

Creeley, Robert, 1926–
    Windows / Robert Creeley.
        p.   cm.
    ISBN 0–8112–1122–3 (alk. paper).—ISBN 0–8112–1123–1 (pbk. : alk. paper)
    I. Title.
PS3505.R43W55   1990
811'.54—dc20   89–13345
                                                    CIP

New Directions Books are published for James Laughlin
by New Directions Publishing Corporation,
80 Eighth Avenue, New York 10011

Contents

For Penelope, Willy, and Hannah

1 THE COMPANY

SONG

What's in the body you've forgotten
and that you've left alone
and that you don't want—

or what's in the body that you want
and would die for—
and think it's all of it—

if life's a form to be forgotten
once you've gone and no regrets,
no one left in what you were—

That empty place is all there is,
and/if the face's remembered,
or dog barks, cat's to be fed.

I WOULD HAVE KNOWN
YOU ANYWHERE

Back of the head, hand, the hair
no longer there, blown, the impotence
of face, the place no longer there, known
you were going to be there—

You were a character of dream,
a mirror looking out, a way
of seeing into space, an
impotent emptiness I share—

This day we spoke as number,
week, or time, this place an
absent ground, a house remembered
then no place. It's gone, it's gone.

What is it sees through, becomes
reflection, empty signal of the past,
a piece I kept in mind because
I thought it had come true?

I would have known you anywhere,
brother, known we were going to meet
wherever, in the street, this echo
too. I would have known you.

THE TERRIBLY STRANGE BED

I recall there being
portraits on the wall
with stiff, painted eyes
rolled round in the dark

on the wall across
from my bed and the other
in the room upstairs
where we all slept

as those eyes kept looking
the persons behind
about to kill me
only in sleep safe.

STAIRWAY TO HEAVEN

Point of hill
we'd come to, small
rise there, the friends
now separate, cars
back of us by
lane, the stones,
Bowditch, etc., location,
Tulip Path, hard
to find on the
shaft, that insistent
rise to heaven
goes down and down,
with names like floors,
ledges of these echoes,
Charlotte, Sarah,
Thomas, Annie
and all, as with
wave of hand I'd
wanted them one
way or other to
come, go with them.

INTERIOR

The room next to
this one with the lowered
lights, the kids watching
television, dogs squatted
on floor, and couch's
disarray, and all that
comes of living anywhere
before the next house, town,
people get to know you if
you let them, nowhere safe.

COMMON

Common's profound bottom
of flotsam, specious increase
of the space, a ground abounds,
a place to make it.

NOT MUCH

Not much you ever
said you were thinking
of, not much to
say in answer.

EPIC

Wanting to tell
a story,
like hell's simple invention, or
some neat recovery

of the state of grace,
I can recall lace curtains,
people I think I remember,
Mrs. Curley's face.

THE WORLD

The world so sweet its
saccharine outshot by
simple cold so colors
all against the so-called
starkness of the winter's
white and grey the
clouds the ice the
weather stables all in
flat particular light
each sunlit place so placed.

AFTER PASTERNAK

Think that it's all one?
Snow's thud, the car's
stuck door, the brilliant,
patient sun—

How many millions of years
has it been coming
to be here just this once—
never returning—

Oh dull edge of prospect—
weary window on the past—
whatever is here now
cannot last.

TREE

for Warren

You tree
of company—

here
shadowed branches,

small,
twisted comfortably

your size,
reddish buds' clusters—

all of
you I love

here
by the simple river.

BROAD BAY

Water's a shimmer,
banks green verge,
trees' standing shadowed,
sun's light slants,
gulls settle white
on far river's length.
All is in a windy echo,
time again
    a far sense.

JUST IN TIME

for Anne

Over the unwritten
and under the written
and under and over
and in back and in front of
or up or down or in
or in place of, of not,
of this and this, of
all that is, of it.

NATIONALGALERIE BERLIN

Nationalgalerie's
minute spasm's
self-reflective—
art's meager agony?

Two hundred years
zap past
in moment's
echoing blast!

No one apparently left
to say "hello"—
but for the genial
late Romanticists.

God, what a life!
All you see is *pain*.
I can't go through *that* again
—gotta go!

•

Trying to get *image of man*
like trying on suit,
too small, too loose,
too late, too soon—

Wrong fit. Wrong time.

And you look out of
your tired head,
still stark naked,
and you go to bed.

•

"Bellevue-Tower"
could be Brooklyn.
The roller skaters
go round and around on the plaza,

like "In Brueghel's great picture, The Kermess . . ."
Their rhythmic beauty
is so human, so human.
I watch and watch.

•

Kids now with skate boards.
Edge of their chatter,
boys. voices changing,
lower, grow harsher.

This is the life of man,
the plans. the ways
you have to do it.
"Practice makes perfect."

•

BY THE CANAL/SITTING

The rippled, shelved
surface of water,
quiet canal, the chunky
horse chestnut trees spread over
reflected in edge of darker
surface where else the light
shows in endless small rows
of slight, securing peace and quiet.

17

Further off, on each side,
cars, buses, trucks, bikes, and people.

But man and boy
pass back of me, spin of wheels,
murmur of their voices.

LIFE

for Basil

Specific, intensive clarity,
like nothing else
is anything
but itself—

so echoes all,
seen, felt, heard
or tasted, the one
and many. But

my slammed fist
on door, asking
meager, repentant entry
wants more.

DIALING FOR DOLLARS

CHOO CHOO

My mother just on edge
of unexpected death the
fact of one operation over
successful says, *it's all
free, Bob! You don't
have to pay for any of it!*
Life, like. Waiting for the train.

•

LIKE MINE

I'll always love
you no matter you
get all that money
and don't need a
helping hand like mine.

•

WAITING

I've never had the
habit of money but
have at times wanted
it, enough to give
myself and friends an
easy time over the
hump but you can
probably keep it, I'm
just here breathing, brother,
not exactly beside you.

•

THE WILLYS

Little
dollar
bills.

PICTURE

The scale's wrong. Kid's
leaned up against
Dad's huge leg, a

tree trunk, unfeeling bark,
rushing waters
of piss? Must be it

smells like toast,
like granular egg
or all night coffee

on all alone. All
so small,
so far to go.

LEAVING

Where to go
if into blank wall
and back of you
you can't get to—

So night is black
and day light,
ground, water
elemental.

It all accumulates
a place, something real
in place.
There it is—

till it's time to go,
like they say,
but the others
want to stay, and will.

NATURE MORTE

It's still
life. It
just ain't moving.

FLEURS

Clumped Clares.
Asphobellies.
Blumenschein.

THE COMPANY

for the Signet Society, April 11, 1985

Backward—as if retentive.
"The child is father to the man"
or some such echo of device,
a parallel of use and circumstance.

Scale become implication.
Place, postcard determinant—
only because someone sent it.
Relations—best if convenient.

"Out of all this emptiness
something must come . . ." Concomitant
with the insistent banality, small, still
face in mirror looks simply vacant.

Hence blather, disjunct, incessant
indecision, moving along on
road to next town where what waited
was great expectations again, empty plate.

So there they were, expectably ambivalent,
given the Second World War
"to one who has been long in city pent,"
trying to make sense of it.

We—*morituri*—blasted from classic
humanistic *noblesse oblige,* all the garbage
of either so-called side, hung on
to what we thought we had, an existential

raison d'être like a pea
some faded princess tries to sleep on,

and when that was expectably soon gone,
we left. We walked away.

Recorders ages hence will look for us
not only in books, one hopes, nor only under rocks
but in some common places of feeling,
small enough—but isn't the human

just that echoing, resonant edge
of what it knows it knows,
takes heart in remembering
only the good times, yet

can't forget whatever it was,
comes here again, fearing this
is the last day, this is the last,
the last, the last.

2 WINDOW

SCALES

for Buddy

Such small dimension
finally, the comfortable
end of it, the people
fading, world shrunk

to some recollected
edge of where it used to be,
and all around a sound
of coming, going. rustle

of neighboring movement out there
where as ever what one finally
sees, hears, wants, waits
still to recognize—is it

the sun? Grass, ground,
dog's bark. bird, the
opening, high clouds, fresh,
lifting day—*someone?*

XMAS

I'm sure there's a world I
can get to by walking another
block in the direction that
was pointed out to me by any-

one I was with and would even
talk to me that late at
night and with everything
confused—I know—the

kids tired, nerves stretched—
and all, and this person, old
man, Santa Claus! by
god—the reindeer, the presents.

WINDOW

THEN

The window had
been half
opened and the

door also
opened, and the
world then

invited, waited,
and one
entered

•

X

The world is
many, the

mind is
one.

•

WHERE

The window
opened,

beyond edge
of white hall,

light faint
shifts from back

a picture?
slurlike "wing"?

Who's
home?

•

The roof's
above, old

reddish dulled
tiles. small

dormered windows, two
chimneys, above

the greyish,
close sky.

•

Who's there,
old
question, who's
here.

•

LIGHT

Light's on
now

in three
sided balcony

window mid-
building, a floor

up from street.
Wait.

Watch it.
What light

on drab earth,
place on earth—

Continue?
Where to go so

far away
from here?

Friends?
Forgotten?

Movement?
A hand just

flesh, fingers?
White—

Who threads fantastic tapestry
just for me, for me?

•

WAITING

One could sit
minutes, hours,

days, weeks,
months, years—

all of its
rehearsal one

after one, be done
at last with it?

      •

Or could go
in

to it, be
inside

head, look
at day

turn to dark,
get rid

of it at last, think
out

of patience, give
it up?

      •

Man
with paper, white,

in hand
"tells the truth"

silent, moves
past the window

away—
sits down?

Comes back,
leans

forward at waist,

somewhat stiffly—
not

old,
young, young.

•

He must love someone
and this must be the story

of how he wanted
everything rightly done

but without the provision
planned, fell forward

into it all,
could not withstand

the adamant simplicity
of life's "lifelike" reality—

even in a mirror
replaced by another—

and couldn't wait
any longer,

must have
moved here.

To "live a life" alone?
to "come home"?

To be "lost and found"
again, "never more to roam"

again. Or something more like
"the fading light," like

they say, never quite
come. Never just one.

PLACE

Your face
in mind, *slow* love,

slow growing, *slow*
to learn enough.

Patience to learn
to be *here,* to savor

whatever there is
out there, without you

here, here
by myself.

NEW WORLD

Edenic land, Adamic person—
Foolishness is the price you'll have to pay
for such useless wisdom.

HO HO

I have broken
the small bounds
of this existence and
am travelling south

on route 90. It
is approximately
midnight, surrogate
earth time, and you

who could, can, and
will never take anything
seriously will die
as dumb as ever

while I alone in
state celestial shoot
forward at designed rate,
speed at last unimpeded.

3   SEVEN

SEVEN: A Suite for Robert Therrien

STRAIGHT

They were going up in
a straight line right
to God, once they died—

The hills of home here
are a yellow pointer, again
God's simplistic finger—

Over the hill, the steeple
still glows in the late light—
all else whited out.

•

PLATE

All I ever wanted was
a place

up there
by myself.

•

"and the sky above—an old

blue

place" an

old

blue plate an old

blue face

·

Very carefully I
cut out an absolute

circle of blue
sky

or water. They
couldn't tell

the difference.

·

Blue plate

special

·

RED

When it goes
that fast

you don't see anything
but speed, you see

red.

·

I got something stuck
in my hand.

It was a splinter.

·

In the first World War
they had bombs

that looked like this.

·

How fast
do you think it's going?

·

SNOWMAN

Help the holes
be bigger. Put

your hand
in.

·

He grew a
point on

top
of his head—

two
of them.

·

That ice
cream cone'll

drip?

•

Curious
key hole.

•

I want to go into the immense
blue yonder

and I've built a negative number
times three.

•

WINGS

Those are hills out there
or mounds

Or breasts filling
the horizon.

•

It's a bird! Such
grace.

•

Sitting here
in Maine

I put you on the window sill
against the blue, white

yellow sky. You're a
sea gull suddenly.

What else
do I want.

      •

Miles away they
are waiting for the promised

land again and the wind
has moved

the sand
into these shapes.

      •

BOX

What do you think
he's got it for

unless
he means to use it.

      •

No way
that could fit

(me)

•

"The worms
crawl in. The"

•

People walked
through the town carrying

coffins!

•

a *coffin*
fit . . .

Heh,
heh.

•

Just stand him up
in the corner.

•

BOAT

Rock me, boat.
Open, open.

Hold me,
little cupped hand.

Let me come in,
come on

board you, sail
off, *sail off* . . .

H'S

Have Hannah's happy health—
have whatever, be

here, hombre . . . Her
hands upon edge

of table, her eyes
as dark centers, her

two teeth—but all,
her climbing, sacklike,

limp, her hands out-
stretched, or simply out

to it, her coming here,
her, all of her, her

words of her, *Hannah,
Hannie.* Good girl,

good. So we go
on with it. So is

Hannah
in this world.

AFTER FROST

for Sherman Paul

He comes here
by whatever way he can,
not too late,
not too soon.

He sits, waiting.
He doesn't know
why he should
have such a patience.

He sits at a table
on a chair.
He is comfortable
sitting there.

No one else
in this room,
no others, no expectations,
no sounds.

Had he walked
another way,
would he be here,
like they say.

BLACK GRACKLE

for Stan and Jane

Black grackle's refreshing eyeblink
at kitchen sink's
wedged window—
a long way to go after all,

a long way back to the crack
in some specific wall
let the light in, so
to speak— Let the bird *speak,*

squeak prettily, and sit
on my finger, pecking ring's blue
stone. Home, home all around here,
geese peer in, goats graze, I suppose

they eat, want no
arbitrary company nor summary
investigation pretends in any way
so to know them—and give milk.

Youth has its own rewards,
and miles to go before I sleep
is echo of miles and miles,
wherever, whatever it was—

I wanted you and *you*
sat down to stay awhile.
If all there was was such
one pulled the threads and all

fell out, if going there was only
coming here with times between

and everyday a holiday with Mary
and *I love you still* and *always will,*

then *then* could not begin again
its busyness, its casual consequences,
and no head on no shoulders, *no
eyes or ears,* etc., nothing forward

in this peculiarly precious instance
scrunched down here, screaming—ultimate *me*—
for miles and miles around
its devastating sound.

THE SEASONS

for Jasper Johns

"Therefore all seasons will be sweet to thee . . ."
—S. T. Coleridge, "Frost at Midnight"

Was it *thunk* suck
of sound an insistent

outside into the patience
abstract waited was lost

in such simple flesh *où*
sont les mother and

father so tall the green
hills echoéd and light

was longer, longer, into
the sun, all the small

body bent at last to
double back into one

and one and one wonder,
paramour pleasure.

•

High air's lightness heat
haze grasshopper's chirr

sun's up hum two close
wet sweat time's hung in space

dust deep greens a wave of grasses
smells grow faint sounds echo

the hill again up and down
we go—

summer, summer, and not even
the full of it . . .

Echoes again body's time a
ticking a faint insistent

intimate skin wants weather
to reassure.

        •

All grown large world
round *ripeness is all*

an orange pumpkin harsh
edge now of frost an

autumnal moon over the
far off field leads back

to the house all's dead
silence the peculiarly

constructed one you were
all by yourself   *Shine on*

Hear the walls of fall
The dark flutes of autumn

sound softly . . . Oh love,
love, remember me.

        •

As if because or
whenever it was it was

there again muffled mute
an extraordinary quiet

white and cold far off
hung in the air without

apparent edge or end
nowhere one was or if

then gone waited
come full circle again

deep and thick and even
again and again

having thought to go nowhere
had got there.

•

The seasons, tallies of earth,
keep count of time,
say what it's worth.

SIGHT

Eye's reach out window water's
lateral quiet bulk of trees at
far edge now if peace were
possible here it would enter.

·

Bulk of trees' tops mass of
substantial trunks supporting from
shifting green base lawn variable
greens and almost yellow looks like.

·

Seven grey metal canoes drawn
up and tethered by pond's long
side with brushy green bushes and
metallic light sheen of water at evening.

·

What see what look for what
seems to be there front of the fore-
head the echoing painful minded-
ness of life will not see this here.

4 DREAMS

DREAMS

What you think you
eat at some table like
a pig with people
you don't even

know and lady there
feeds you all and you,
finally you at least
are full, say, look at

them still eating! Why
(says a woman, another
sitting next to me) those
others still eating you

so cannily observed are
unlike you who *could* be fed
because you were hungry! But
them, they can't—they

are possessed by the
idea of hunger, *never* enough
to eat for them, agh . . .
Or you either, dreamer,

who tells this simple
story being all these
same offensive persons
in one empty head.

•

In dreams begin the
particulars of those
echoes and edges,

the quaint ledges of
specific childhood nailed
to my knees and

leaning in unison
while the other
men went off, the

women working, the
kids at baleful
play, mud-colored

with rocks and stones and
trees years ago in
Albuquerque, New Mexico we'd

stopped the night I dreamt
I was to be child forever
on way to get the kids from camp.

•

Have you ever
had vision as if

you were walking
forward to some

edge of water through
the trees, some country

sunlit lane, some
place was just ahead

and opening as your body
elsewise came

and you had
been in two places?

FOR THE WORLD THAT EXISTS

No safer place to live than with children
for the world that exists.

IF

Up the edge of the window out to
tree's overhanging branches sky
light on facing building up to
faint wash blue up on feet ache
now old toes wornout joints make
the wings of an angel so I'd fly.

LIGHTS

I could get
all of it.

I could say
anything.

I wish I could
just get even.

I'm here.
I'm still here.

When did
it happen.

Where was
everyone.

I wish I could
just get even.

Now you've
gone away.

Nobody
wants to stay.

Here I am.
Here I am.

I DREAMT

I dreamt I dwelt in a big building—
four walls, floor and a ceiling,
bars in front and behind.
Nothing on my mind

I dreamt I dwelt in a can,
round, tin, sides, top and bottom,
and I couldn't get out.
Nobody to get me out.

I dreamt I dwelt in marble halls,
a men's room with a trough
you pissed in, and there I was.
There were a lot of us.

I dreamt I dwelt in a house,
a home, a heap of living
people, dogs, cats, flowers.
It went on for hours.

Whatever you dream is true.
It's just you making it up,
having nothing better to do.
Even if you wanted to, you couldn't.

SPARKS STREET ECHO

Flakes falling
out window make
no place, no place—

no faces, traces,
wastes of whatever
wanted to be—

was here
momently, mother,
was here.

YOU

You were leaving, going
out the door in

preoccupation as to
what purpose it

had served, what
the point was, even

who or what or where,
when you thought you

could, suddenly, say
you understood, and

saw all people as if
at some distance, a

pathetic, vast huddle
up against a fence.

You were by no means
the Cosmic Farmer

nor Great Eyeball in Sky.
You were tired, old now,

confused as to purpose,
even finally alone.

You walked slowly
away or rather got in

the car was waiting
with the others.

How to say clearly what
we think so matters

is bullshit, how all the
seeming difference is none?

Would they listen, presuming
such a *they?* Is any-

one ever home to such in-
sistences? How ring

the communal bell?
All was seen in

a common mirror, all
was simple self-

reflection. It was me
and I was you.

FOCUS

Patches of grey
sky tree's

lines window
frames the

plant hangs
in middle.

PLAGUE

When the world has become a pestilence,
a sullen, inexplicable contagion,

when men, women, children
die in no sense realized, in

no time for anything, a
painful rush inward, isolate—

as when in my childhood the
lonely leper pariahs so seemingly

distant were just down the street,
back of drawn shades, closed doors—

no one talked to them, no one
held them anymore, no one waited

for the next thing to happen—as
we think now the day begins

again, as we look for the faint sun,
as they are still there, we hope, and we are coming.

AGE

Most explicit—
the sense of trap

as a narrowing
cone one's got

stuck into and
any movement

forward simply
wedges one more—

but where
or quite when,

even with whom,
since now there is no one

quite with you—   Quite? Quiet?
English expression: *Quait?*

Language of singular
impedance? A dance? An

involuntary gesture to
others *not* there? What's

wrong here? How
reach out to the

other side all
others live on as

now you see the
two doctors, behind

you, in mind's eye,
probe into your anus,

or ass, or bottom,
behind you, the roto-

rooter-like device
sees all up, concludes

"like a worn out inner tube,"
"old," prose prolapsed, person's

problems won't do, must
cut into, cut out . . .

The world is a round but
diminishing ball, a spherical

ice cube, a dusty
joke, a fading,

faint echo of its
former self but remembers,

sometimes, its past, sees
friends, places, reflections,

talks to itself in a fond,
judgmental murmur,

alone at last.
I stood so close

to you I could have
reached out and

touched you just
as you turned

over and began to
snore not unattractively,

no, never less than
attractively, my love,

my love—but in this
curiously glowing dark, this

finite emptiness, *you, you, you*
are crucial, hear the

whimpering back of
the talk, the approaching

fears when I may
cease to be me, all

lost or rather lumped
here in a retrograded,

dislocating, imploding
self, a uselessness

talks, even if finally to no one,
talks and talks.

FUNNY

Why isn't it funny when you die,
at least lapse back into archaic pattern,
not the peculiar holding on to container
all other worlds were thought to be in—

archaic, curious ghost story then,
all sitting in the familiar circle,
the light fading out at the edges,
and voices one thinks are calling.

You watch them go first, one by one,
you hold on to the small, familiar places,
you love intently, wistfully, now
all that you've been given.

But you can't be done with it
and you're by no means alone.
You're waiting, watching them go,
know there's an end to it.

5 EIGHT PLUS

IMPROVISATIONS

for Lise Hoshour

YOU BET

Birds like
windows.

•

YONDER

Heaven's up
there still.

•

THE KIDS

Little
muffins

in a
pan.

•

THE CART

Oh well, it
thinks.

•

NEGATIVE

There's a big
hole.

·

SITE

Slats in
sunlight a
shadow.

·

PURITAN

Plant's in
place.

·

VIRTUES

Tree limbs'
patience.

·

CARS

Flat out
parking lot.

·

BLUE

Grey blue
sky blue.

·

HOLES

Sun's
shining through

you.

•

TEXAS REVERSE

You all
go.

•

ECHOES

"All god's
children got—"

•

OLD SONG

"Some sunny
day—"

•

YEAH

Amazing grace
on Willy's face!

•

HELP

This here
hand's out.

·

SEE

Brown's another
color.

·

DOWN

It's all
over
the floor.

·

WINDOW

Up from reflective
table top's glass the
other side of it.

·

AROUND

The pinwheel's pink
plastic spinning
blade's reversing.

·

EGO

I can
hear I can
see

·

DAYTIME

It's got to be
lighter.

•

SPACE

Two candles
light brown—
or yellow?

•

WINDOW SEAT

Cat's up
on chair's edge.

•

EYES

All this
color's yours.

•

GREEN

Plant's tendrils
hanging from

but not
to—

•

SEASCAPE

Little boat
blue blown
by bay.

•

BIT

"De
sign ~~Qu~~
art
e[a]rly"

•

CROUP

"AL
APHIC
Y"

•

WEIGH

Rippled refractive
surface leaves
light lights.

•

THE EDGE

"Your
Mem
Is Enc

·

QUOTE

"a lot
  of thought-
  ful people"

·

GHOST

What you don't
see you
hear?

·

TEACHER

The big
red
apple.

·

CANDLE HOLDER

Small glass
cube's opaque
clarity in
window's light.

·

FIELDS

Meadows
more at home.

87

·

TABLE TOP

Persian's
under glass.

WHEELS

for Futura 2000

One around one—
or inside, limit
and dispersal.

Outside, the emptiness
of no edge, round
as the sky—

Or the eye seeing
all go by
in a blur of silence.

OH

Oh stay awhile.
sad, sagging flesh
and bones gone brittle.

Stay in place,
aged face, teeth,
don't go.

Inside and out
the flaccid change
of bodily parts,

mechanics of action,
mind's collapsing
habits, all

echo here
in mottled skin, blurred eye,
reiterated mumble.

Lift to the vacant air
some sigh, some sign
I'm still inside.

READING OF EMMANUEL LEVINAS

"He does not limit knowledge
nor become the object of thinking . . ."
　　　　　　—Krzystztof Ziarek

Thought out of self
left beyond the door

left out at night
shuttered openness

dreams dream of dreaming
inside seeming outside

since left then gone
comes home alone.

　　　•

Puts hands down
no river one place

step over into
the ground sense

place was will be
here and now

nowhere can be
nothing's left.

　　　•

Outside forms distance
some hundred feet

away in boxed air across
bricked enclosed space

a horizontal young woman
blue coat red pants

asleep on couch seen
through squared window

five floors up in form
above's blue sky

a lateral cloud
air of solemn thinking.

•

Who else was
when had they come

what was the program
who was one

why me there
what other if

the place was determined
the deed was done?

WATER

Your personal world echoes
in ways common enough,
a parking lot, common cold,
the others sitting at the table.

I have no thoughts myself,
more than myself. I feel
here enough now to think
at least I am here.

So you should get to
know me? Would I be
where you looked? Is it
hands across this body of water?

Is anyone out there,
they used to say, or was
they also some remote chance
of people, a company, together.

What one never knows is,
is it really real, is
the obvious obvious, or else
a place one lives in regardless.

CONSOLATIO

What's gone is gone.
What's lost is lost.

What's felt as pulse—
what's mind, what's home.

Who's here, where's there—
what's patience now.

What thought of all,
why echo it.

Now to begin—
Why fear the end.

WHAT

What would it be
like walking off
by oneself down

that path in the
classic woods the light
lift of breeze softness

of this early evening and
you want some time
to yourself to think

of it all again
and again an
empty ending?

SENATOR BLANK BLANK

I look at your
bland, piglike
face and hear

your thin-lipped,
rhetorical bullshit
and wonder if anyone

can or will believe you,
and know they do,
just that I'm listening to you too.

BETTER

Would it be better
piecemeal, a little
now and then, or

could one get inside
and hide there, wait
for it to end.

No one's doing anything to you.
It's just there's nothing
they can do for you.

Better with dignity to die?
Better rhetoric would clarify.
"Better Business Bureaus" lie.

WALL

You can push as hard as you want
on this outside side.

It stays limited
to a single face.

USA

Seeing with Sidney people
asleep on floor of subway—

myself worrying about time—
how long it would take to get to the plane—

How far in the universe to get home,
what do you do when you're still alone,

what do you say when no one asks,
what do you want you don't take—

When train finally comes in,
there's nothing you're leaving, nothing you can.

FOR AN OLD FRIEND

What became of your novel with the lunatic
mistaken for an undercover agent,

of your investment of the insistently vulnerable
with a tender of response,

your thoughtful wish that British letters
might do better than Peter Russell—

Last time I saw you, protesting
in London railway station

that all was changed,
you asked for a tenner

to get back to Bexhill-on-Sea.
Do you ever think of me.

HERE

In other
words opaque
disposition intended
for no one's interest
or determination
forgotten ever
increased but
inflexible and
left afterwards.

EARS IDLE EARS

for Susan

Out one
ear and
in the
other ear
and out
without it.

BLUE MOON

The chair's still there,
but the goddamn sun's
gone red again—

and instead of Mabel
there is a potato,
or something like that there,

sitting like it owned the place.
It's got no face
and it won't speak to anyone.

I'm scared.
If I had legs,
I'd run.

ECHO

Rudimentary characteristic of being
where it has to be, this tree

was where it was
a long time before anything else

I know or thought to.
Now it's pushed out by people—

rather by their effects, the weakening
the insistent wastes produce.

Where can anyone go
finally if the damn trees die

from what's done to them—what
being so-called *alive* has come to?

What's left after such death.
If nothing's there, who's here.

FAMOUS LAST WORDS

for John Chamberlain

PLACE

There's a way out
of here but it

hurts at the edges
where there's no time left

to be one if
you were and friends

gone, days seemingly
over. No one.

•

LATE

Looks like chunks
will be it
tonight, a bite-sized

lunch of love,
and lots of it,
honey.

•

VERDE

Green, how I love you green . . .
the prettiest color I've ever seen,

the way to the roses through them stems,
the way to go when the light changes!

What grass gets when you water it,
or the folding stuff can get you in,

but finally it's what isn't dead
unless it's skin with nothing under it—

or faces green from envy or hunger or fear,
or some parallel biological fact, my dear.

.

BOZO

Bill's brother was partial
to windows, stood on boxes

looking over their edges.
His head was

higher than his shoulders,
but his eyes were

somewhere down under
where he thought he could

see it all now, all
he'd wanted to, aged four,

looking up under skirts,
wearing ochre-trim western shirts.

Regular slim-jim ranchero,
this vicious, ambitious, duplicitous, no

wish too late, too
small, bozo.

•

MILES

Simple trips, going
places, wasted
feelings, alone
at last, all the rest

of it, counting, keeping
it together, the weather,
the particular people, all
the ways you have to.

•

NIGHT LIGHT

Look at the light
between the lights

at night with the lights
on in the room you're sitting

in alone again with
the light on trying still

to sleep but bored and
tired of waiting up late

at night thinking of some
stupid simple sunlight.

•

ECHOES (1)

Patience, a peculiar
virtue, waits in time,

depends on time to
make it, thinks it

can have everything
it wants, wants all

of it and echoes dis-
appointment, thinks

of what it thought
it wanted, nothing else.

·

ECHOES (2)

This intensive going in,
to live there, in

the head, to wait
for what it seems

to want, to look
at all the ways

of looking, seeing
things, to always

think of it, think
thinking's going to work.

·

LIFE

All the ways to go,
the echoes, made sense.

It was as fast as that,
no time to figure it out.

No simple straight line,
you'd get there in time

enough standing still.
It came to you

whatever you planned to do.
Later, you'd get it together.

Now it was here.
Time to move.

·

FAMOUS LAST WORDS

Which way did they go?
Which way did they come.

If it's not fun, don't do it.
But I'm sure you wouldn't.

You can sum it all up in a few words
or less if you want to save time.

No wisdom hasn't been worn out
by simple repetition.

You'll be with me till the end?
Good luck, friend.

ECHOES

for William Bronk

The stars stay up there where they first were.
We have changed but they seem as ever.

What was their company first to be, their curious proposal,
that we might get there which, of course, we did.

How dead now the proposal of life simply, how echoing it is,
how everything we did, we did and thought we did!

Was it always you as one, and them as one,
and one another was us, we thought, a protestant, a complex

determination of this loneliness of human spaces.
What could stars be but something else no longer there,

some echoing light too late to be for us specific.
But there they were and there we saw them.

EIGHT PLUS

Inscriptions for Eight Bollards
at 7th & Figueroa, LA

for James Surls

What's still here settles
at the edges of this
simple place still
waiting to be seen.

•

I didn't go
anywhere and
I haven't
come back!

•

You went by so
quickly thinking
there's a whole world
in between.

•

It's not a
final distance,
this here
and now.

•

How much I would
give just to know

you're standing in
whatever way here.

•

Human eyes
are lights to me
sealed
in this stone.

•

No way to
tell you anything
more than
this one.

•

You walk tired
or refreshed, are
past in a moment,
but saw me.

•

Wish happiness
most for us,
whoever we are,
wherever.

•

If I sit here
long enough,
all will pass me by
one way or another.

•

Nothing left out,
it's all in a heap,
all the people
completed.

•

Night's eye is
memory
in day-
light.

•

I've come and gone from here
with no effect,
and now feel
no use left.

•

How far from
where it
was I'll
never know.

•

You there
next to the others
in front of
the one behind!

•

No one speaks
alone. It
comes out
of something.

•

Could I think
of all you
must have felt?
Tell me.

•

What's inside,
what's the place
apart from
this one?

•

They say this
used to be
a forest
with a lake.

•

I'm just
a common
rock,
talking.

•

World's
still got

four
corners.

.

What's
that
up there
looking down?

.

You've got a nice
face and
kind eyes and
all the trimmings.

.

We talk like
this too
often someone
will get wise!

6   HELSINKI WINDOW

"Even if he were to throw out by now absolutely incomprehensible stuff about the burning building and look upon his work simply as an effort of a carpenter to realize a blueprint in his mind, every morning he wakes up and goes to look at his house, it is as if during the night invisible workmen had been monkeying with it, a stringer has been made away with in the night and mysteriously replaced by one of inferior quality, while the floor, so meticulously set by a spirit level the night before, now looks as if it had not even been adjudged by setting a dish of water on it, and cants like the deck of a steamer in a gale. It is for reasons analogous to this perhaps that short poems were invented, like perfectly measured frames thrown up in an instant of inspiration and, left to suggest the rest, in part manage to outwit the process."

—Malcolm Lowry, *Dark As the Grave Wherein My Friend Is Laid*

X

The trees are kept
in the center of the court,
where they take up room
just to prove it—

and the garbage cans extend
on the asphalt at the far side
under the grey sky and the building's
recessed, regular windows.

All these go up and down
with significant pattern,
and people look out of them.
One can see their faces.

I know I am safe here
and that no one will get me,
no matter where it is
or who can find me.

HELP

Places one's come to
in a curious stumble, things
one's been put to, with,
in a common bundle

called suffering humanity
with faces, hands
where they ought to be,
leaving usual bloody traces.

I like myself, he thought, but
it was years and years ago
he could stand there watching
himself like a tv show.

Now you're inside entirely,
he whispers in mock self-reassurance,
because he recognizes at last, by god,
he's not all there is.

SMALL TIME

Why so curiously happy
with such patient small agony,
not hurting enough
to be real to oneself—

or even intimidated
that it's at last too late
to make some move
toward something else.

Late sun, late sun,
this far north you still shine,
and it's all fine,
and there's still time enough.

BIENVENU

for the company of Lise Hoshour, Phi-
lippe Briet, Michel Butor, and Robert
Therrien: "7&6," Philippe Briet Gallery,
NYC, October 7, 1988

Welcome to this bienfait
ministry of interior muses,
thoughtful provocateurs, etc.

All that meets your eye
you'll hear with ear
of silent surprises

and see these vast surmises
bien entendu by each
autre autrefois. Our

welcome so to you
has come— Mon frère, mon semblable,
and sisters all.

•

Thoughtful little holes in
places makes us
be here.

Empty weather makes
a place of faces
staring in.

Come look at
what we three
have done here.

"EVER SINCE HITLER . . ."

Ever since Hitler
or well before that
fact of human appetite
addressed with brutal
indifference others
killed or tortured or ate
the same bodies they
themselves had we ourselves
had plunged into density
of selves all seeming stinking
one no possible way
out of it smiled or cried
or tore at it and died
apparently dead at last
just no other way out.

THINKING

I've thought of myself
as objective, viz.,
a thing round which
lines could be drawn—

or else placed by years, the average
some sixty, say, a relative
number of months, days,
hours and minutes.

I remember thinking of war
and peace and life
for as long as I can remember.
I think we were right.

But it changes, it thinks
it can all go on forever
but it gets older.
What it wants is rest.

I've thought of place
as how long it takes
to get there and of where
it then is.

I've thought of clouds, of water
in long horizontal bodies, or
of love and women and the children
which came after.

Amazing what mind makes
out of its little pictures,
the squiggles and dots,
not to mention the words.

CLOUDS

The clouds passing over, the
wisps still seeming substantial, as
a kid, as a kid I'd see them up there

in the town I grew up in on the hills
in the fields on the way home then
as now still up there, still up there.

ALL WALL

Vertical skull time
weather blast bombastic disaster impasse time,
like an inside out and back down again design,
despair ready wear impacted beware scare time—

like old Halloween time,
people all gone away and won't be back time,
no answer weeks later empty gone out dead
a minute ahead of your call just keeps on ringing time—

I'm can't find my way back again time,
I'm sure it was here but now I can't find it time,
I'm a drag and sick and losing again wasted time,
You're the one can haul me out and start it over again

Time. Too much time too little
not enough too much still to go time,
and time after time and not done yet time
nothing left time to go time. Time.

WHATEVER

Whatever's
to be
thought
of thinking
thinking's
thought of
it still
thinks
it thinks
to know
itself so
thought.

.

Thought so
itself know to
thinks it
thinks still it
of thought
thinking's
thinking
of thought
be to
whatever's.

KLAUS REICHERT AND
CREELEY SEND REGARDS

in memory L.Z.

Nowhere up there enough
apart as surmised see my
ears feel better in the
air an after word from Romeo's
delight spells *the* and *a*
aged ten forever friend
you'll know all this by heart.

ECHOES

What kind of crows,
grey and black, fussy
like jays, flop
on the tree branches?

"What kind of
love is this" flops
flat nightly, sleeps
away the days?

What kind of place
is this? What's out there
in these wet unfamiliar
streets and flattened,

stretched faces?
Who's been left here,
what's been wasted
again.

FOOLS

1

Stripped trees in the wet wind,
leaves orange yellow, some still green,
winter's edge in the air,
the close, grey sky . . .

Why not be more
human, as they say,
more thoughtful,
why not try to care.

The bleak alternative's
a stubborn existence—
back turned to all,
pathetic resistance.

2

You'd think the fact
another's tried it
in the common world
might be a language

like the animals
seem to know
where they've come from
and where they'll go.

Curse the fool
who closes his sad door—
or any other more
still tries to open it.

MEAT

Blood's on the edge of it
the man with the knife cuts into it

the way out is via the door to it
the moves you have mean nothing to it

but you can't get away from it
there's nothing else left but it

have you had enough of it
you won't get away from it

this room is thick with it
this air smells of it

your hands are full of it
your mouth is full of it

why did you want so much of it
when will you quit it

all this racket is still it
all that sky is it

that little spot is it
what you still can think of is it

anything you remember is it
all you ever got done is always it

your last words will be it
your last wish will be it

The last echo it last faint color it
the drip the trace the stain—it.

NEW YEAR'S RESOLUTION

What one might say
wanting to do it,
hoping to solve it,
make resolution—

You break it to bits,
swallow the pieces,
finally quit quitting,
accept it, forget it.

But what world is this
has such parts,
or makes even thinkable
paradoxic new starts—

Turn of the year
weighs in the cold
all that's proposed
simply to change it.

Still, try again
to be common, human,
learn from all
how to be one included.

THE DRUNKS OF HELSINKI

Blue sky, a lurching tram makes
headway through the small city.
The quiet company sits shyly,
avoiding its image, else talks

with securing friends. This
passage is through life as if
in dream. We know our routes
and mean to get there. Now

the foetid stink of human excess,
plaintive, and the person beside us
lurches, yet stays stolidly there.
What are the signals? Despair,

loss of determinants—or a world
just out of a bottle? Day
after day they clutter the tram
stops, fall sodden over seats

and take their drunken ease in
the fragile world. I think, they
are the poets, the maledictive,
muttering words, fingers pointing,

pointing, jabbed outright across
aisle to blank side of bank or
the company's skittish presence.
I saw a man keep slamming the post

with his fist, solid in impact,
measured blows. His semblable sat
slumped in front of me, a single seat.
They meet across the aisle in ranting voices,

each talking alone. In a place of
so few words sparely chosen, their
panegyric slabbering whine has human
if unexpected resonance. They

speak for us, their careful friends, the sober
who scuttle from side to side in vacantly
complex isolation, in a company has compact
consensus, minds empty of all conclusion.

HELSINKI WINDOW

for Anselm Hollo

Go out into brightened
space out there the fainter
yellowish place it
makes for eye to enter out
to greyed penumbra all the
way to thoughtful searching
sight of all beyond that
solid red both brick and seeming
metal roof or higher black
beyond the genial slope I
look at daily house top on
my own way up to heaven.

•

Same roof, light's gone
down back of it, behind
the crying end of day, "I
need something to do," it's
been again those other
things, what's out there,
sodden edge of sea's
bay, city's graveyard, park
deserted, flattened aspect,
leaves gone colored fall
to sidewalk, street, the end
of all these days but
still this regal light.

•

Trees stripped, rather shed
of leaves, the black solid trunks up

to fibrous mesh of smaller
branches, it is weather's window,
weather's particular echo, here
as if this place had been once,
now vacant, a door that had had
hinges swung in air's peculiar
emptiness, greyed, slumped elsewhere,
asphalt blank of sidewalks, line of
linearly absolute black metal fence.

•

Old sky freshened with cloud bulk
slides over frame of window the
shadings of softened greys a light
of air up out of this dense high
structured enclosure of buildings
top or pushed up flat of bricked roof
frame I love *I love* the safety of
small world this door frame back
of me the panes of simple glass yet
airy up sweep of birch trees sit in
flat below all designation declaration
here as clouds move so simply away.

•

Windows now lit close out the
upper dark the night's a face
three eyes far fainter than
the day all faced with light
inside the room makes eye re-
flective see the common world
as one again no outside coming
in no more than walls and post-
card pictures place faces across

that cautious dark the tree no
longer seen more than black edge
close branches somehow still between.

.

He was at the edge of this
reflective echo the words blown
back in air a bubble of suddenly
apparent person who walked to
sit down by the familiar brook and
thought about his fading life
all "fading life" in tremulous airy
perspect saw it hover in the surface
of that moving darkness at the edge
of sun's passing water's sudden depth
his own hands' knotted surface the
sounding in himself of some other.

.

One forty five afternoon red
car parked left hand side
of street no distinguishing
feature still wet day a bicycle
across the way a green door-
way with arched upper window
a backyard edge of back wall
to enclosed alley low down small
windows and two other cars green
and blue parked too and miles
and more miles still to go.

.

This early still sunless morning when a chair's
creak translates to cat's cry a blackness still

out the window might be apparent night when the
house still sleeping behind me seems a bag of
immense empty silence and I feel the children
still breathing still shifting their dreams an
enigma will soon arrive here and the loved one
centers all in her heavy sleeping arm out the
leg pushed down bedclothes this body unseen un-
known placed out there in night I can feel all
about me still sitting in this small spare pool of
light watching the letters the words try to speak.

.

Classic emptiness it
sits out there edge of
hierarchic roof top it
marks with acid fine edge
of apparent difference it
is *there* here *here* that
sky so up and out and where
it wants to be no birds no
other thing can for a
moment distract it be
beyond its simple space.

WHAT

What had one thought the
outside was but place all
evident surface and each
supposed perspect touched
texture all the wet implicit
world was adamant edge of
limit responsive if indifferent
and changing (one thought) in-
side its own evident kind one
banged upon abstract insens-
itive else echoed in passing
was it the movement one's own?

VOICE

Bears down on
the incisive way to
make a point common
enough speaking
in various terms it
says the way of
satisfaction is a
lowly thing echo
even wants to can
come along alone in-
clusion also a way
particularizing life.

SO MUCH

When he was a kid sick
in bed out the window
the clouds were thick and
like castles, battlements he'd
think he could climb up to
them, a veritable jack in
the beanstalk high there with
sun and blue air he'd never
need anything more again to
get well, so it had to fade
away, whatever that old voice
enlarges, so much to depend upon.

ECHO

for J. L.

Outside the
trees
make limit of
simple

sight. The
weather is
a grey, cold on
the

skin. It feels
itself
as if a place it
couldn't

ever get to
had been at
last
entered.

WINTER NIGHT

Building's high bulk lifts
up the mass is lighter in this
curiously illumined darkness air
somehow fragile with the light is
beyond again in yellow lit win-
dows frame of the bars and behind
a seeming room the lamp on the
table there such peculiar small
caring such signs five floors up
or out window see balcony's iron
frame against snowed roof's white
or pinkish close glow all beyond.

FADING LIGHT

Now one might catch it see it
shift almost substantial blue
white yellow light near roof's edge
become intense definition think
of the spinning world is it as
ever this plate of apparent life
makes all sit patient hold on
chute the sled plunges down ends
down the hill beyond sight down
into field's darkness as time for
supper here left years behind waits
patient in mind remembers the time.

OLD MISTER MOONLIGHT

Split broken un-
circumvented excised
walked out door snow
day freaking thoughts
of empty memory back
past time gone undone
left car side pool
of greying edged
rings fledged things
wedged buildings all
patterns and plans fixed
focus death again.

FOR J. L.

The ducks are gone
back to the pond, the echo

of it all a curious
resonance now it's

over, life's like that?
What matters, so soon become fact.

NIGHT

This bluish light behind the block of
building this familiar returning
night comes closer this way can sit
looking see the bulk of it take shape
in front of the sky comes now up from
behind it up to mount its light its
yellow quiet squares fix a front in
the dark to be there make a static
place looks like home in dark's
ambivalence sit down to stay awhile
places there black's dominance a shade it
rides to closes it shuts it finally off.

MARCH

Almost at the dulled
window fact the wet
birches soften in melt-
ing weather up still from
far ground the backyard
asphalt grey plastic garbage
bins the small squat
blackened pile of stubborn
snow still sit there echo
of fading winter all the days
we waited for this side
of spring changes everything.

FIRST LOVE

Oh your face is there a mirror days
weeks we lived those other places in
all that ridiculous waste the young we
wanted not to be walked endless streets
in novels read about life went home at
night to sleep in tentative houses left
one another somewhere now unclear no per-
sons really left but for paper a child or
two or three and whatever physical events
were carved then on that tree like initials
a heart a face of quiet blood and somehow
you kept saying and saying an unending pain.

SPRING LIGHT

Could persons be as this
fluffed light golden spaces
intent airy distances so up
and out again they are here
the evening lowers against the sun
the night waits far off at the
edge and back of dark is summer's
light that slanting clarity all
wonders come again the bodies open
stone stillness stunned in the silence
hovering waiting touch of air's edge
piece of what had not been lost.

INDEX OF TITLES